REVERE BEACH STORIES

POEMS BY
KEVIN CAREY AND JENNIFER MARTELLI

PHOTOGRAPHS BY STEPHENIE YOUNG

RED NUN PRESS
ALLSTON, MAASSACHUSETTS

Red Nun Press is an imprint of Nixes Mate dedicated to publishing books that navigate the connections between photographs and literature.

ISBN 978-1-949279-59-7

Red Nun Press
POBox 1179
Allston, MA 02134
nixesmate.pub/red-nun

...I have found I am where

I am by

being only there,

by standing

in the clouded presence of

the things I observe.

Philip Levine

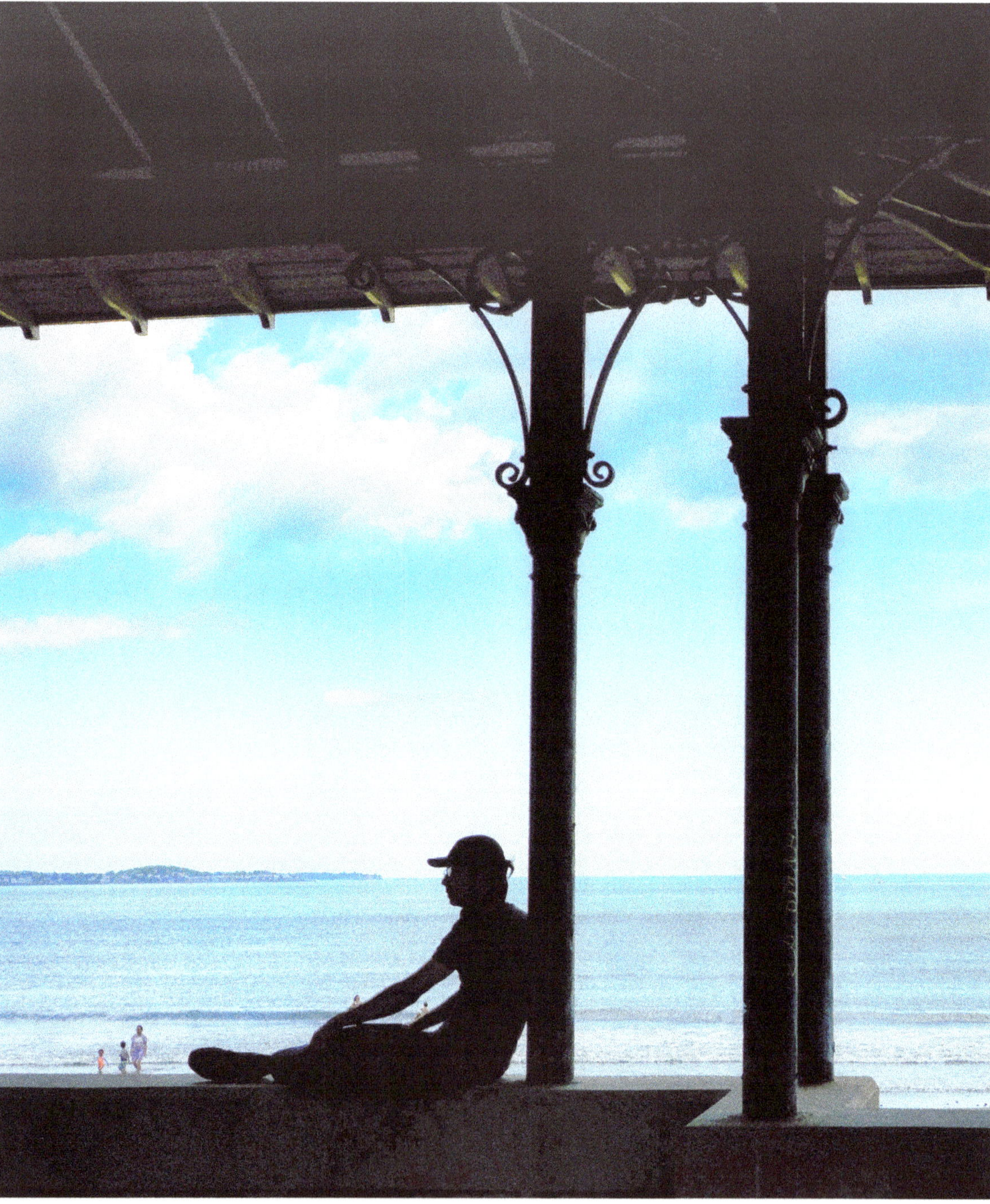

In the shadow of the Boston skyline, Revere Beach, Massachusetts, is a life in pictures: the natural blue ocean horizon, the restaurants and the bars, the cars cruising up and down, the teenagers in packs on hot summer days, the retired folks walking the boardwalk. This urban beachfront also houses many poetic stories: a honky-tonk history, a revolving door of immigrants, gangsters and gamblers, and an often-crowded boulevard teeming with beachgoers from surrounding cities.

Poets Kevin Carey and Jennifer Martelli grew up in Revere in the 1960s. They've both written extensively about this city and its three-mile beachfront, which is the first public beach in America. Stephenie Young, a Somerville photographer, is originally from California. During the Covid epidemic, Young was drawn to this local East Coast ocean and its unfamiliar culture. Thus began a long-term photo project about everyday life in the beach city. After a chance conversation over those photographs and a few poems, this collaboration was born.

This collection attempts to capture the complicated nature of Revere Beach, with the combination of a newcomer's eye and the personal reflections of these poets who have history here. Often overlooked by metropolitan Boston, Revere Beach is not Cape Cod or Nantucket, and that's part of what makes it unique. Through still images and poetry, this book paints a portrait of a place that has influenced each of these artists in a profound way and it gives voice to an often-forgotten urban beach culture in a way that has not been done before.

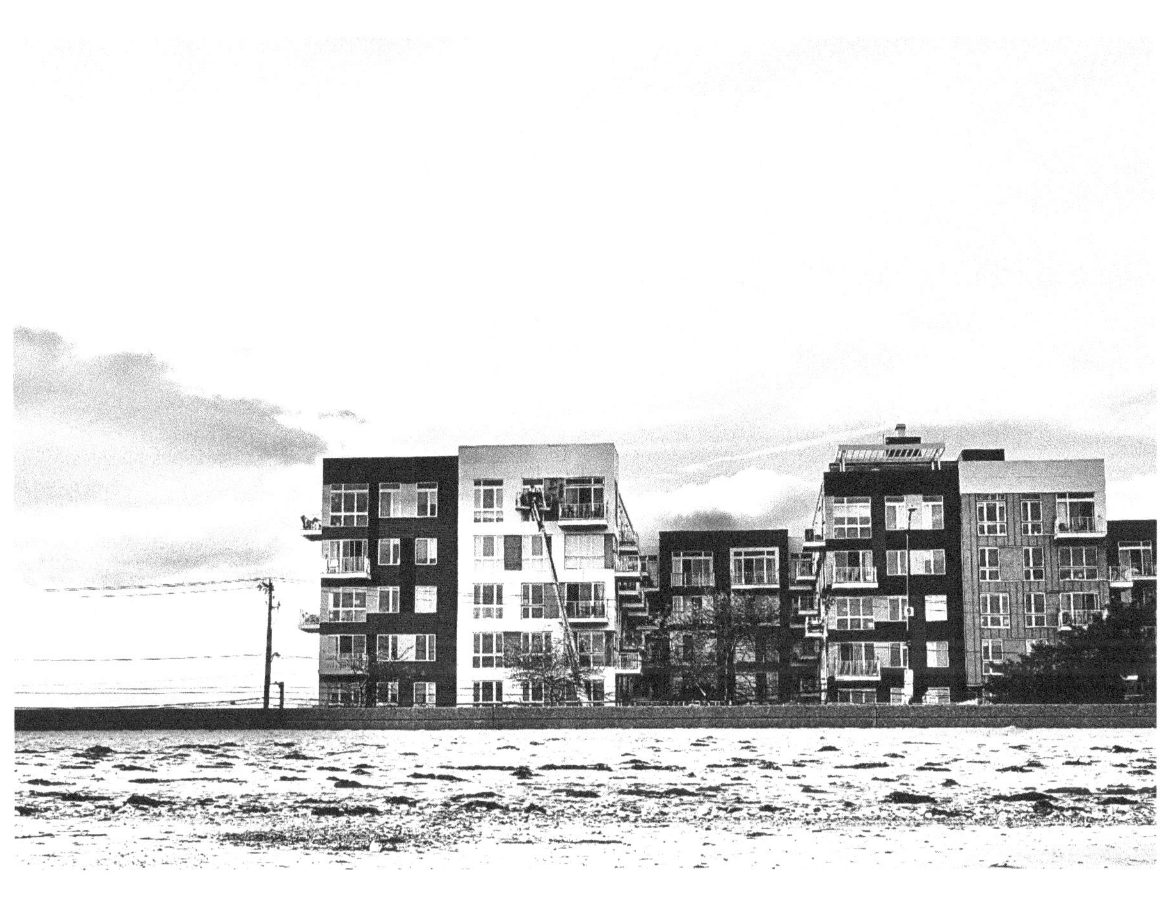

THE RECIPE   [KC]

There's a recipe to beach life: the salt air, the fried food,
the suntan lotion, the traffic, the kids drinking beer on the
seawall, the seagulls picking through trash, the girls from
the Ave in cut-off jeans, the hot August nights. Beach people
know there is something driving them to do the things they do,
they see it in the storms and the waves, in the high and low tides,
when the water washes up over the sea wall in winter and the
sea smoke dances off the ice packs. They see it in the fall when
the fog rolls thick and in the summer when the sun burns like gold
off the still blue glass and they wear sunglasses everywhere
they go. They know they can't ever get away from it. It's in the
blood, like the salt is in the water, it's in the spray and the
seaweed and the sand and the first chill of stepping into the
icy blue water in April.

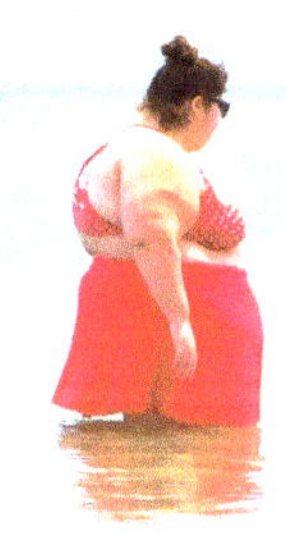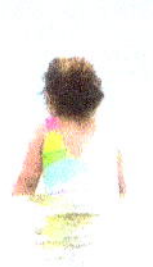

THE DEVIL TIDES [JM]

There are rocks off the coast shaped like eggs. There are rocks shaped like misery and one like a skull. If you are born up here, you know sadness and you know gulls. You know how a good clamshell makes a good ashtray. You know the land is as flat as any place where men change into wolves under the moon. You know that. Resent everything, for it's the only way you don't forget. Resent everything you love, it keeps you anchored to the beach. Some days, the seaweed is red-clogged with pennies or fingers. It smells even in the cold. Too many villages are connected by thin causeways pinched on either side by the Atlantic. Devil tides cut them off from the world. Folks go out and never come back. There are empty graves engraved in marble in big churches. Folks go out hot and turn blue. No one ever forgets, except how to measure. If you knew this, you'd never ask anything more of me.

Any midnight and the beach could still be
cooking with gas, headlights from one end
to the other, muffled hip hop from tinted
windows, a Harley or two weaving in and
out of the traffic, the city skyline looming.
You watch it go by, out the barroom door,
out the takeout stand window. No sense
heading home. No one to go to, just this
beach, the people who work it, who play
on it, the people who don't smell you or
look you up and down because you have
sawdust on your shoes, the walking talking
fish plate, the French-fried human onion
ring. Mr. Invisible stamping two inches
of flour off your high cut sneakers. The
beach brings you all together, a long line
of accumulated misery. Throw a few back,
that's the ticket. Put it on ice, I'll get to it. And
then some, the comfortable sway back in
the legs, the one that makes you think you
can dance and shit if it don't go down better
after eight hours in the box. But there's
always work in the morning, cooking to do,
bums to wait on, like the disco ball says,
more more more.

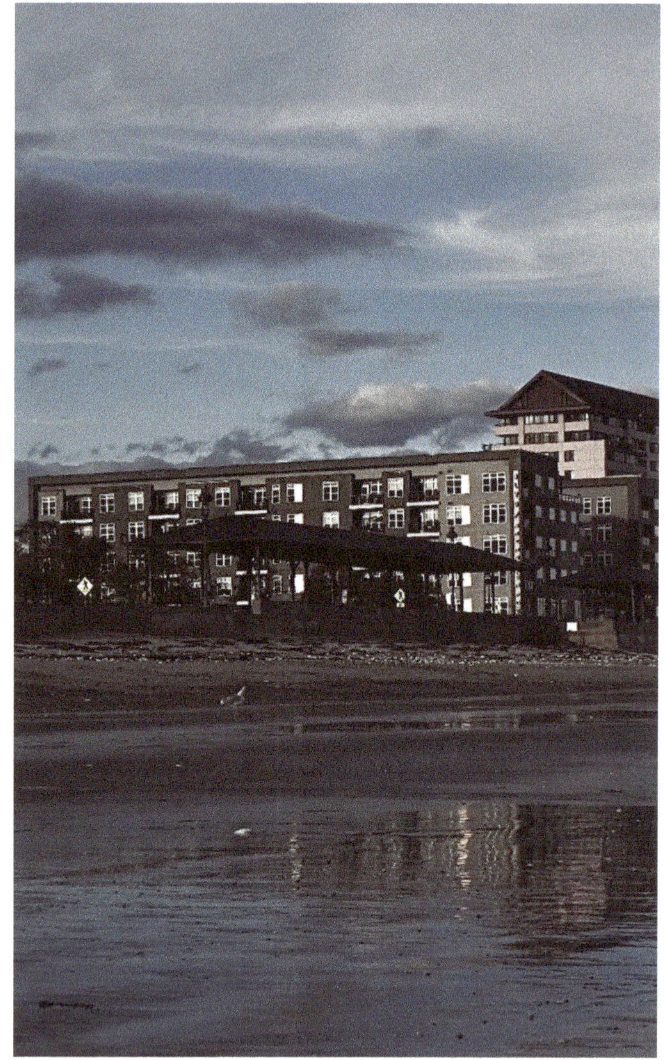

THE BEACH PEOPLE DOING BEACH THINGS   [KC]

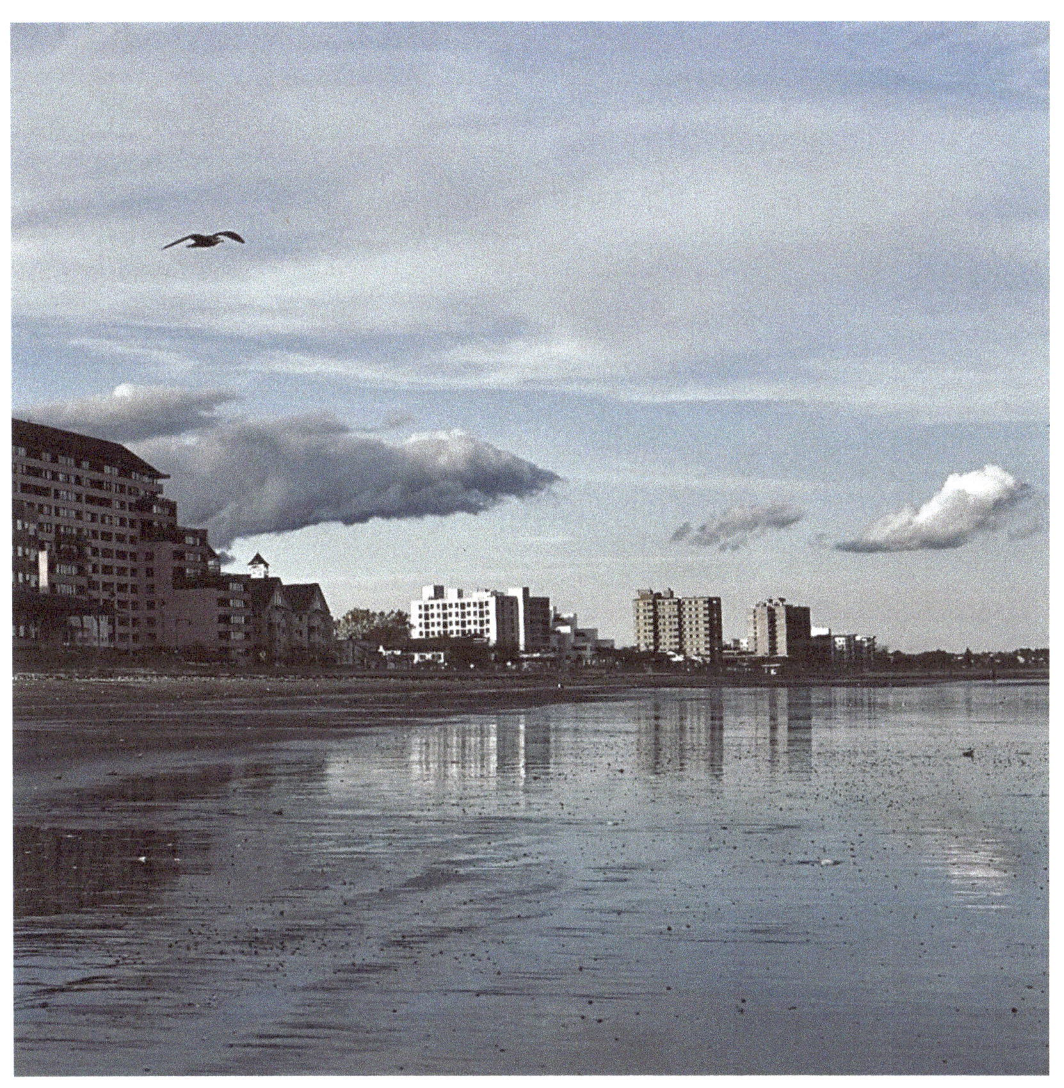

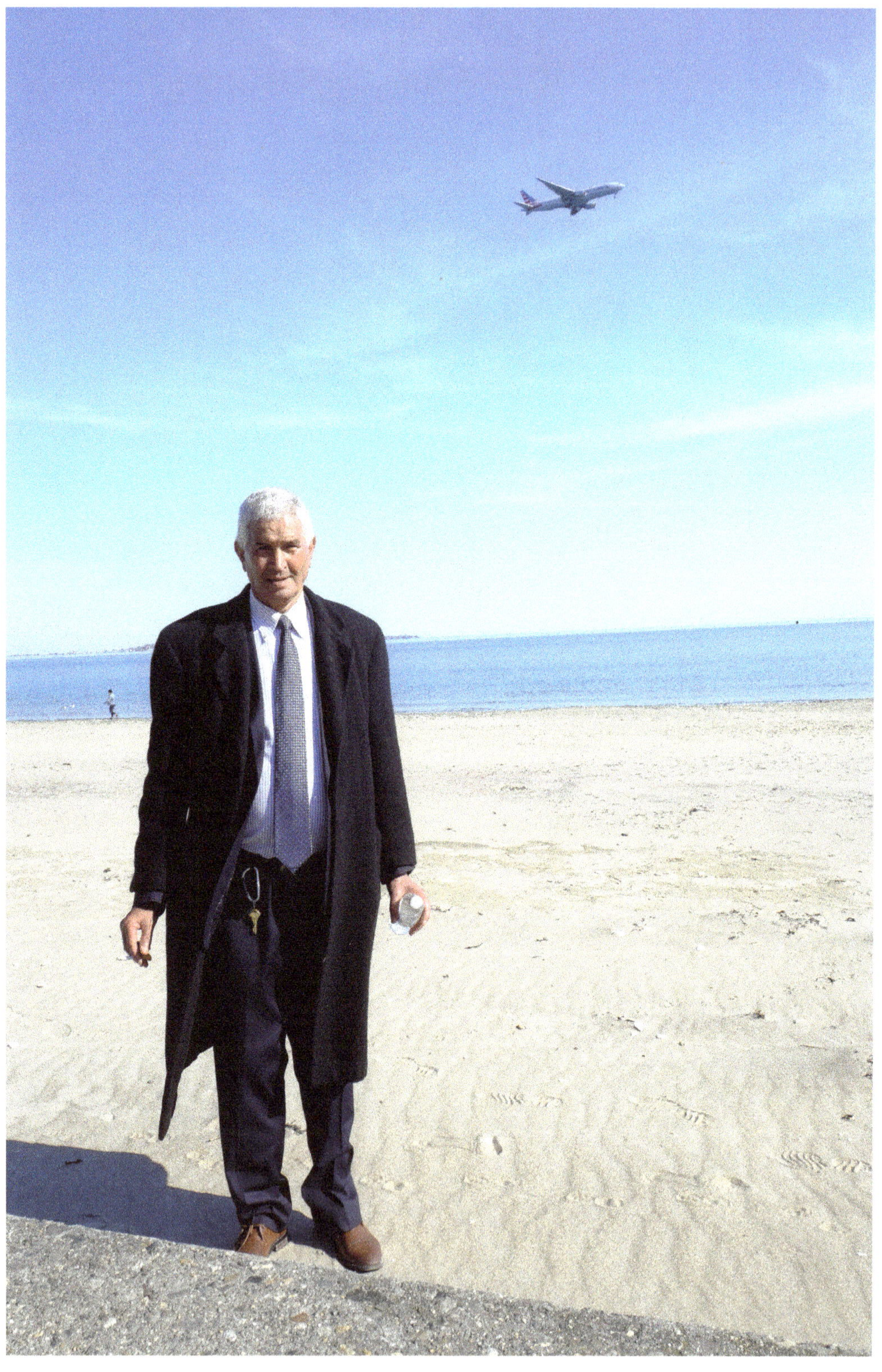

ALWAYS [KC]

I was a function room bartender, weekends on the beach
in the 80's. Always the same scene: young men in ties
reaching for the flying garter belt, a band with a singer
who had sideburns and a ruffled shirt, the best man
sneaking back from the boy's room wiping powder off
his nose, the sweet square old ladies shaking it to the
hully gully – the puffy hair, the tall neck bottles of beer,
the pink gin fizzes, and one happy red-faced uncle
setting up the bar again, *Give 'em all one* and always
there was one wild guy doing a split in the middle of
the dance floor, spilling his drink and bumping into
everyone around him, and always I'd see him at the end
of the night, his shirttail out, sweat stained, smoking a
cigarette, the bride and groom long gone, the band packed
up on the highway home, the house lights bright.
He'd be talking to a bridesmaid or somebody's sister
about a job he lost or about how he missed his kids,
but that he was going to see them soon, and always
this guy would wander over while I was wiping bottles
or counting the cash drawer. He'd smile and ask me if
I had one on ice, which I always did, and he'd lay
a ten down on the bar and salute, like I'd handed him
a secret only the two of us knew.

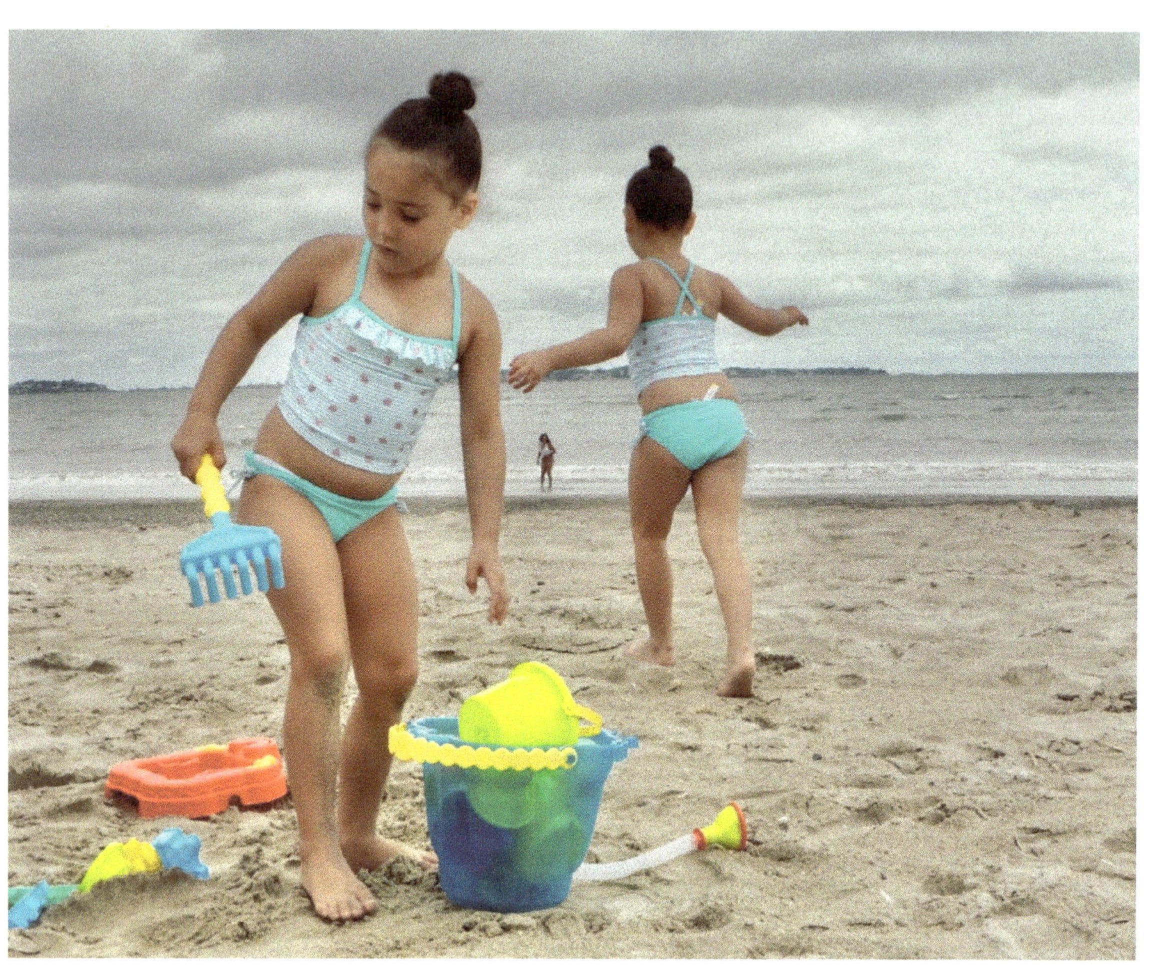

Once they charged to see a train wreck on Side
Beach, watched horses diving thirty feet into a pool,
paid five cents to look at premature babies
in incubators. As a teenager I saw the last
remnants of the arcades, one wooden
roller coaster they tried ten times to burn
to the ground, and the rotating neon line
of barrooms – *the Ebb Tide, the Mickey Mouse,
Sammy's Patio,* the rock and roll, the disco,
the punk, the bikers, the strippers, the wise guys.

But once when I was six years old, I walked
with my father at low tide, the Nahant beach causeway
on one side, the staggered Boston buildings on the other,
a plane flying low to Logan Airport. We held hands and stepped
over the rigged mounds of packed sand, the scattered
strands of seaweed brushing my ankles, the salt air,
the smell of sun-tan lotion, the seagulls. We walked
to the edge of the channel, the boats an arm's length away,
the neighborhood behind us in the distance. I remember it was late
in the day, the sun hazy and starting down. We stood
looking back at the tiny houses, the neat, lined streets,
until the water rose slowly around our legs,
the small cool waves pushing us home, and somewhere out of
sight, I heard the faint chimes of an ice-cream truck.

I have always lived by the ocean. When I was a child, I built my altar at low
tide on Revere Beach. I made a pentacle with:

1.   a small, suede fringe pouch I stole from one sister with my other sister's
     doll tucked inside
2.   the blue plastic pirate sword I pulled from the heart of a Maraschino cherry
3.   grandpa's skeleton key I found dangling from a hook on grandma's stove
4.   from my mother's pocket, the book of matches from The General Edward's Inn
5.   my father's tarnished brass tie pin with an embossed tiny White House.

What I conjured then, I live with now. I conjured women nobody heard.
I asked my friend, who has the same name as I, *do people think I'm not so bright?*
No one thinks that, she said, *but you have a strong accent.*

Long ago, everybody I knew had last names like mine, all ending with a long,
rounded vowel. Vowels have heft. Like planets orbiting, they are frictionless,
compulsive, and smooth. The vowel is the nucleus of a word. Everything – all
sound– depends on the position of the tongue root for articulation, for movement.

Maybe people hear me and think I've never left this place. There are whole sounds I elide,
delete, and erase. There are whole periods of time. too. There are people. What I mean is
no one taught me to: pronounce a whole phoneme, to roll my tongue, to open the glottis, to
think that ghosts won't appear when I speak.

TONGUE ROOT [JM]

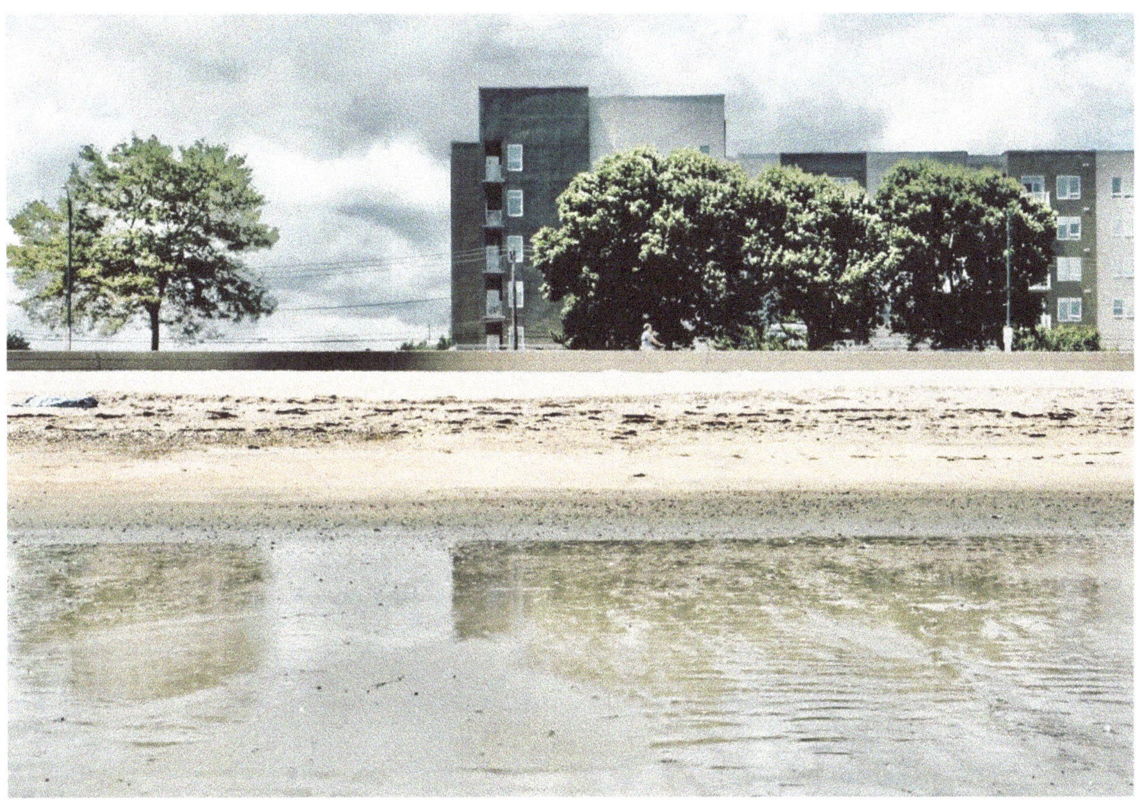

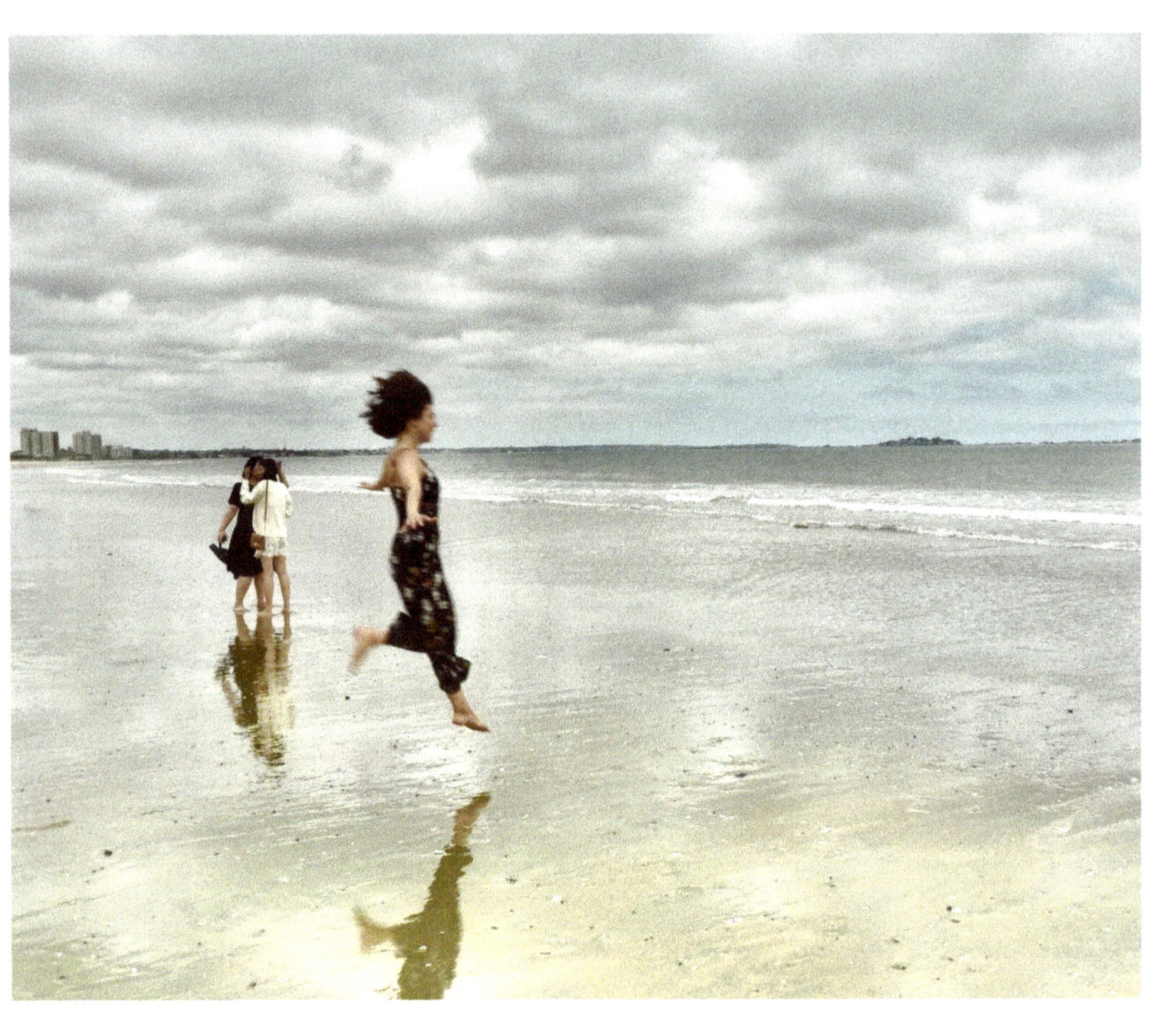

That long-gone summer when I stood upright on my board and paddled around the tide pools
on Revere Beach, above the hermit crabs scuttling over purple rocks looking for new
homes, below the planes landing, coming back, so low I could see their metal bellies,
I cut through the hot solstice air, my balance steady enough I could look over my tan shoulder,
back to the beach: kids, some crying, a small dog chased a gull fat with fried food, & I think
now I was happy, or if not happy, nothing fed this low-tide heart of mine. I remember it was
mid-year and I had yet to give back even an inch of light.

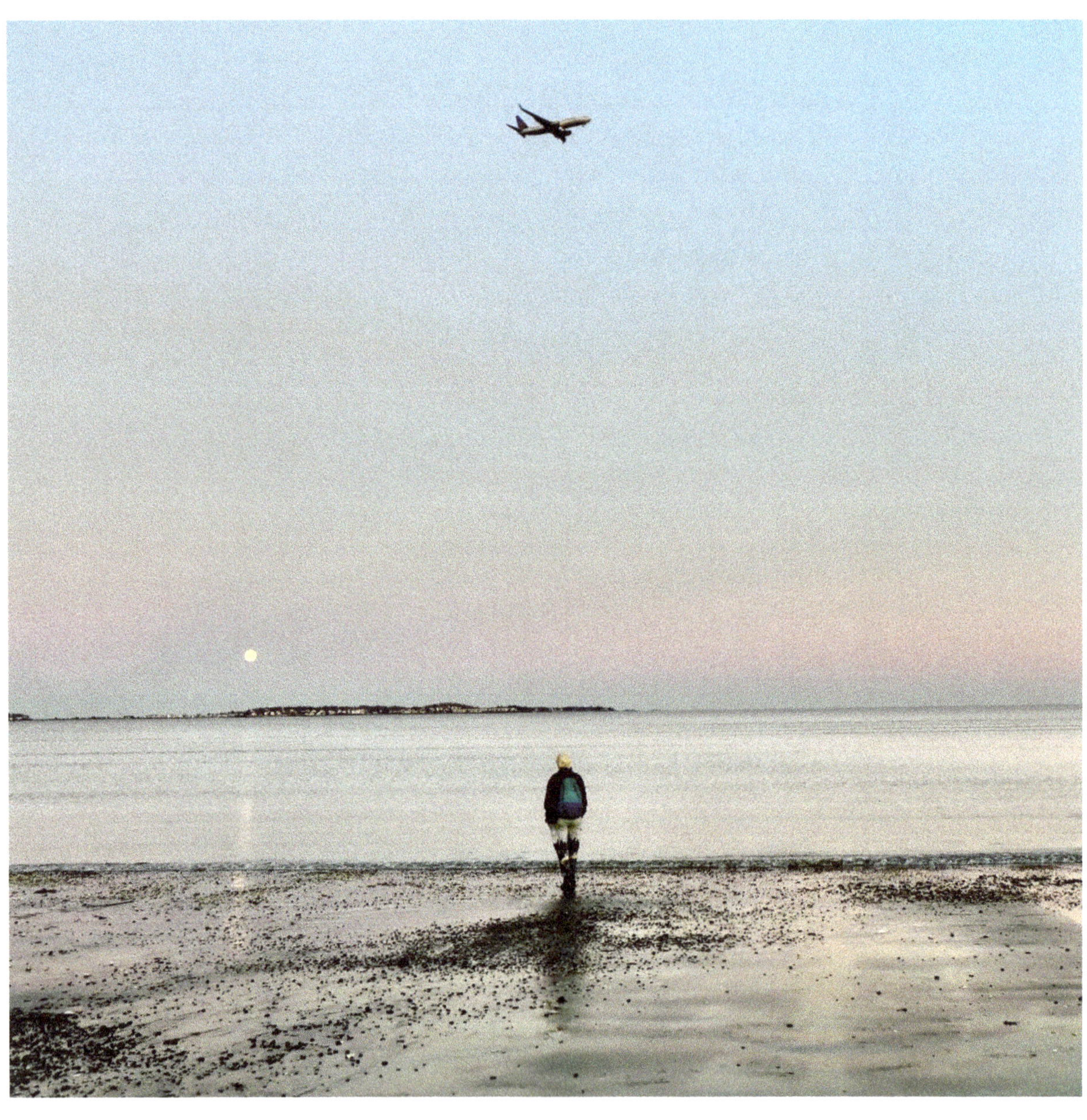

AS A CROW FLIES   [JM]

On my car's navigational system North Shore Road is a straight yellow line between the blue of Revere Beach and the Pines River (where a woman once walked into and drowned herself after shooting her husband at home, and I thought, *what willpower, to drown oneself, to keep going farther in and under*). I am technically on Route 1 which would take me right down to Key West if I kept going for days, as a crow flies. Airplanes lower above me towards Logan, landing, so low people here need shatter-proof windows to muffle the sound and to keep the panes whole.

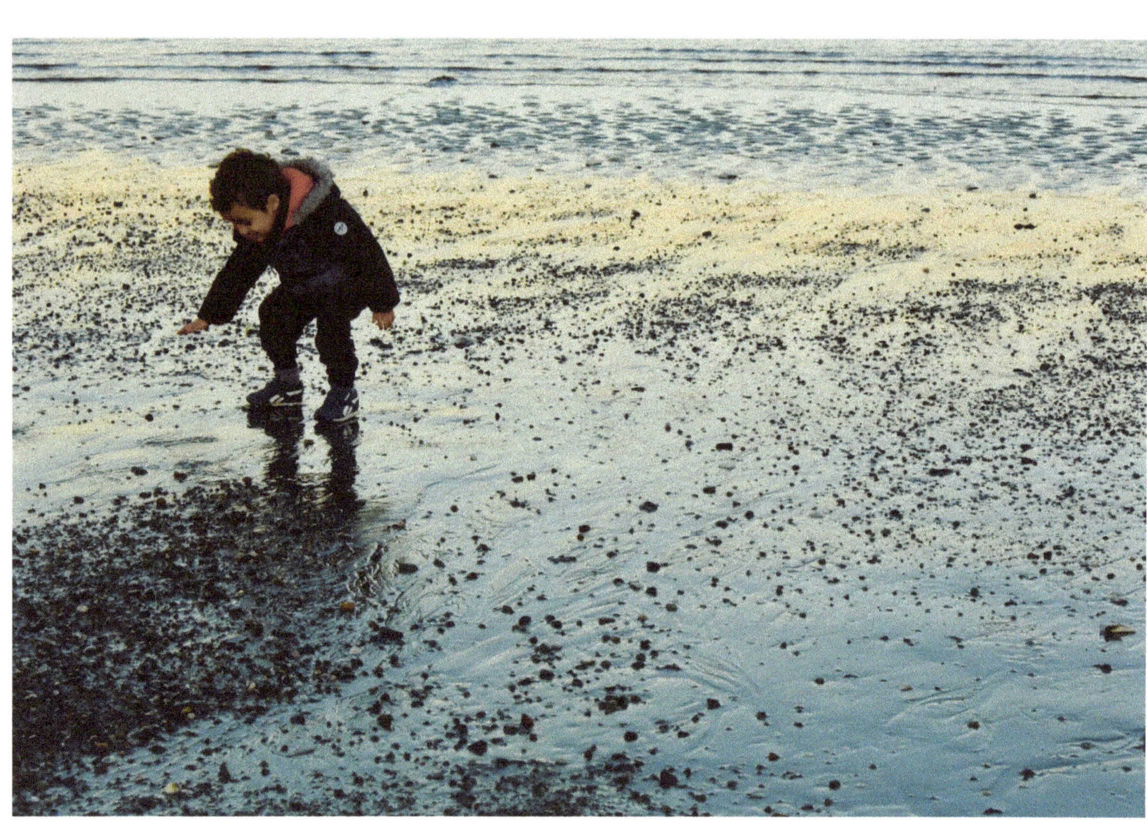

I SLEEP IN THE DAYTIME

"Life During Wartime," Talking Heads

Yesterday, in my half-lucid dream, this: two pearls just outside the bedroom window. I know they were my parents. I had watched a movie deep into that night when time stopped mattering: all the angels in heaven were sent by God to destroy us – they came down the road, the sky was a dark ocean. (Believe me, the women who've come to me in my poems hold my parents deep within their bones – and now I must keep still in my sadness).

The coastline where I live is shaped like a hook for miles. I walked the whole beach at low tide. Washed-up rocks made a moonscape: some white and speckled like the eggs of a great reptile, some rusted tigers' eyes, some smooth, iridescent.

[JM]

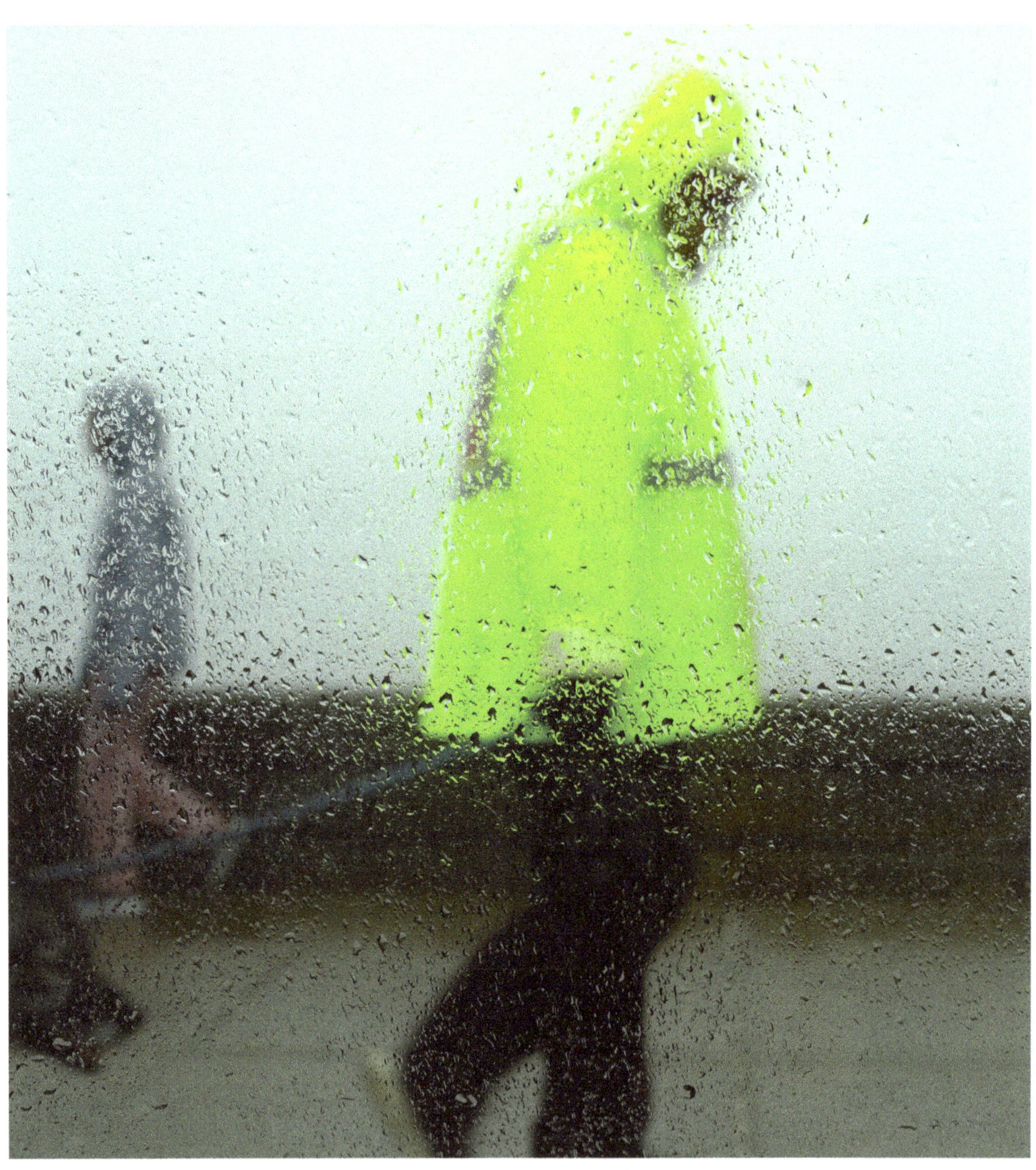

STRANGERS [KC]

I watch the man in the leather jacket
smoking a cigarette against the sea wall,
a slice of graffiti cut off in mid-thought.
He seems disturbed by my presence,
the smoke around him like an aura
of gray dusk, a few empty beer cans at his feet.
He doesn't know I once walked this beach
with a pocket full of quarters to play skeeball,
saw a boy with an eye patch dropping
a switchblade into an empty beer bottle,
doesn't know my uncle would have gotten shot
tending bar if he hadn't run to the racetrack,
or that my friend Donny was killed by a car (eventually)
crossing the boulevard a hundred yards from here.
The water at the man's back is more blue
this time of year, the sand less white than summer,
the same loud motorcycles cruising up and down,
the same neon lights jumping out of the twilight.
He flicks his cigarette to the ground
and walks away and I want to tell him
there is nowhere on the beach he can hide.
Maybe he would agree with me if I said,
the beach makes strangers of us all.

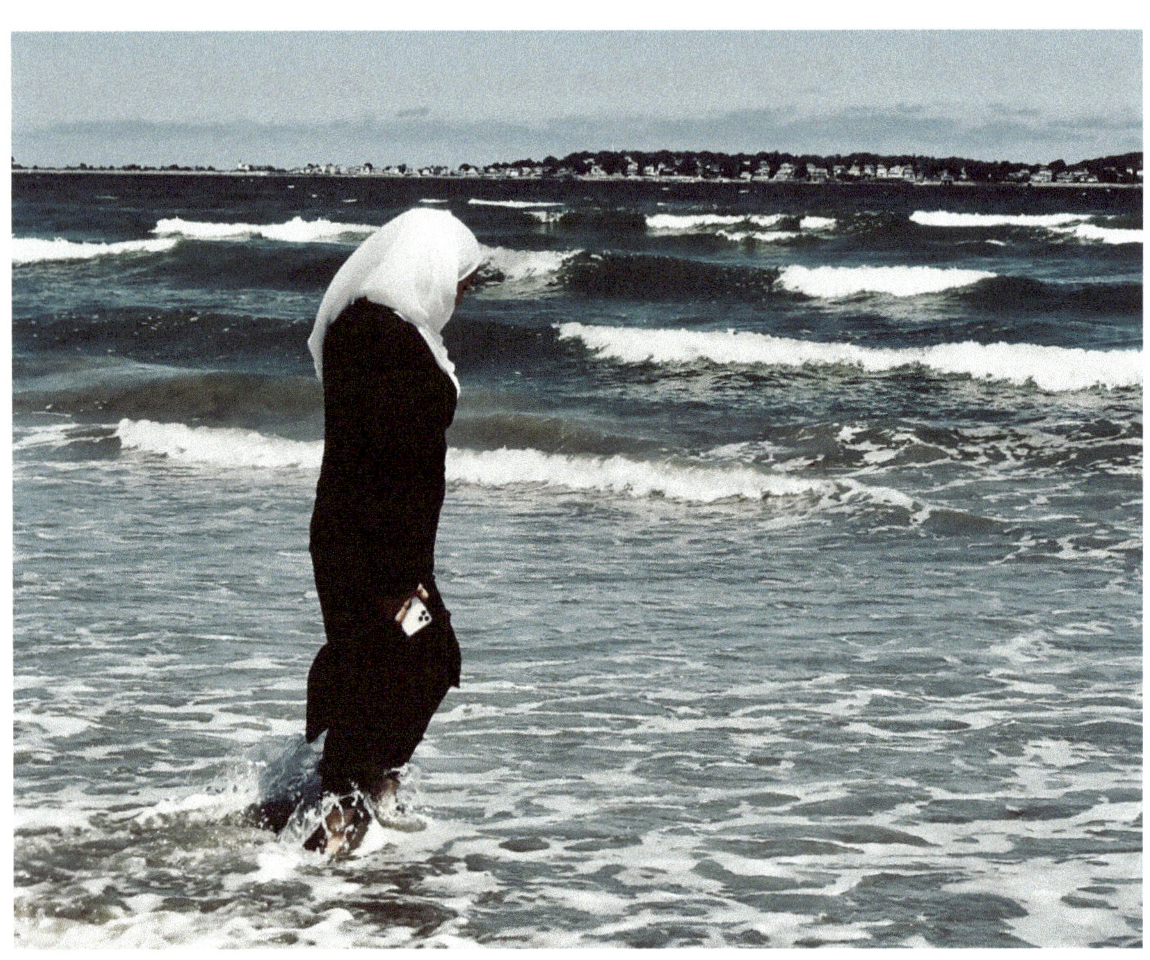

THE VEILED WOMEN   [JM]

walking along Broadway from the bakery and sometimes, the new burqa
store, got my father nervous. I'd drive him by the Beach, by St. Theresa's:
well, I won't be going there anymore, he'd point, screwed by God, by my mother's
Alzheimer's, his cancer: he was going to die and my mother would not know.
The Church sold off St. Theresa's to pay for legal fees and the stone cross was
pulled down like the statue of Saddam Hussein: roped and toppled. A woman
waits out front, so veiled all I see are her eyes, like my own black coon cat. Her
eyes don't scare me, though: if you live here long enough, no one will meet
your gaze. My father hated cats, too. *A man may die once he has married three
daughters off,* Rumi said. My two sisters and I feed our cats until they are fat.
My own cat's fur grows long and she sits waiting, covered and purring, her
eyes green or golden, kissing me with her eyes, warm and plump under fur
that covers her all over.

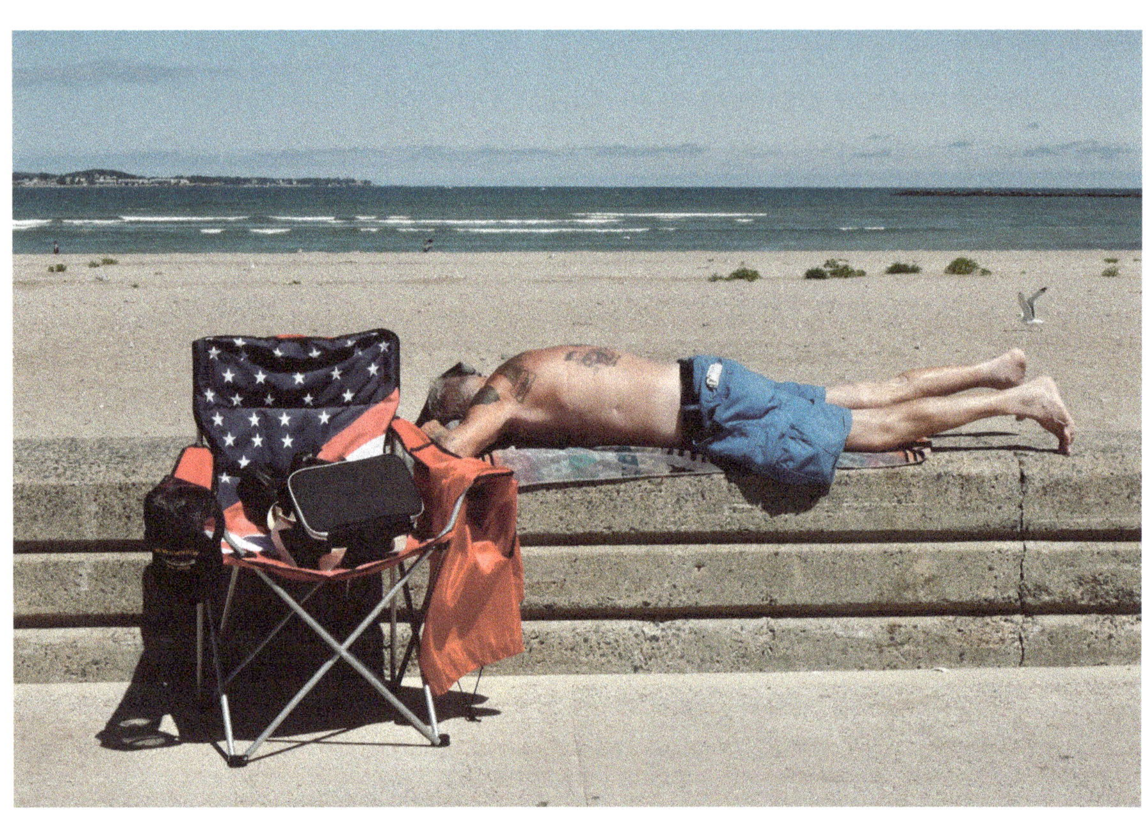

A LONG LINE [KC]

I come from a long line of beach front vendors
caramel popcorn hawkers bartenders fry cookers
a long line of coffee pushers Crackerjack stumpers
cheeseburg makers a long line of saw-dust footed
hotdog dragging cigarette smoking liquor-swabbing
drink men a long line of weary waiters thumping home
after 8 hours in the box 3 am tired-eyed half-in-the-wrapper
drink pourers a long line of sidewalk sweepers cash collectors
grill scrapers counter wipers ash tray emptying straw box
stuffing roast beef slicing French fry bag stacking barroom
bouncing beach bums another long day another short buck
hawk it loud and proud friend long days long nights
a long line of late-day sleepers.

METAMORPHOSIS [JM]

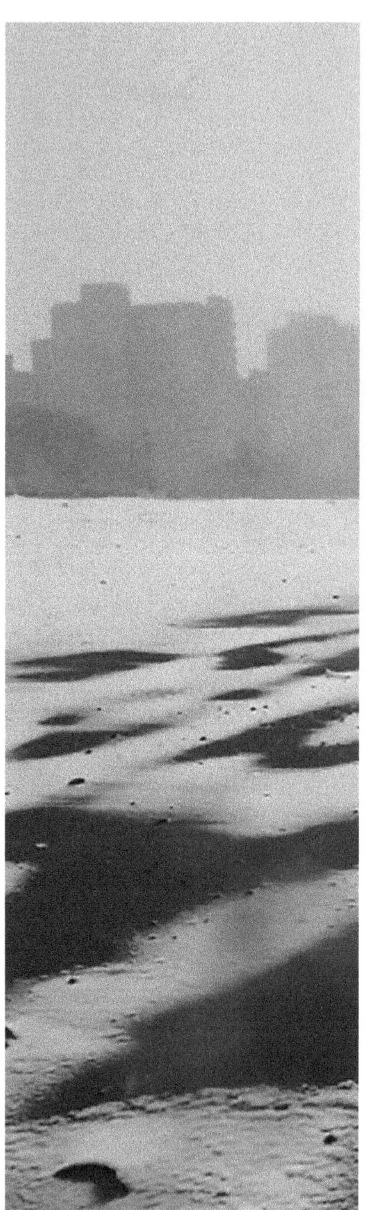

A man came toward me with a giant spool of orange waxy twine
as I walked the Boulevard along the beach, facing Nahant. He
held it as he walked, let it unspool between his hands, tied it
to stakes along the sea grass and beach plums to slow down
erosion on these rooted dunes. I waved, not to him, but to
Sylvia Plath's Egg Rock and bean-green Atlantic, waved to all
her anger and vengeance and joy.

I would love this man's job. If I could walk, unspool, and save
something, I'd walk in my new clogs, the gold ones with wings,
and insist I was a minor god who granted mercies and limits.
I'd unspool the length of a life, smooth it out, or cut it with the
long shears dangling from my waist. I'd tell you to burn nutmeg
and pennyroyal and rue.

I am the god they find deep in the caves, etched next to owls
– I'm the big-eyed one. I'm the figure dug up from a ruin, my
holes made with sticks. Or, I'm the one lying across the curve of
a chipped clay bowl used to catch wine or blood: see? the crude
outline of my spool? the wings at my feet? my long blades?

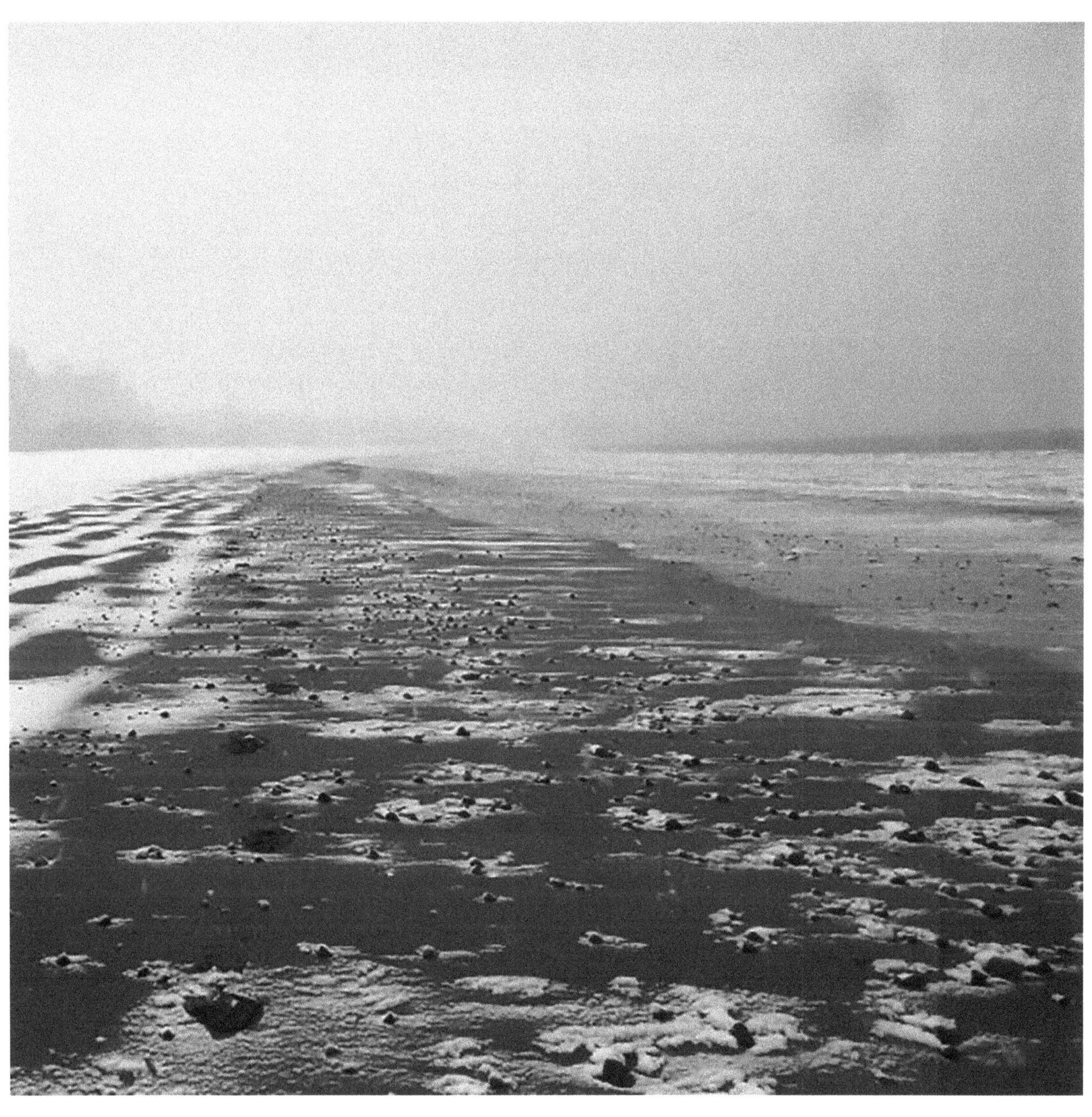

BIOS

Kevin Carey is Coordinator of Creative Writing at Salem State University. Books include: *The Beach People (2014)* Red Bird Chapbooks, *The One Fifteen to Penn Station (2012)*, *Jesus Was a Homeboy (2016)* which was an Honor book for the Paterson Literary Prize, & *Set in Stone (2020)* all from CavanKerry Press. His poems have appeared on *The Writers Almanac on National Public Radio* and on *The Academy of American Poets Poem a Day.* Kevin is also a playwright and a filmmaker. He has co-directed & co-produced two documentaries about poets, *All That Lies Between Us* (about New Jersey poet Maria Mazziotti Gillan) and *Unburying Malcolm Miller*, which premiered at the Massachusetts Poetry Festival in 2017. A crime novel, *Murder in the Marsh*, from Darkstroke Books, was released in October (2020). A new middle grade novel *Junior Miles and the Junkman* dropped in September of 2023 from Regal House / Fitzroy Books, and a new co-written collection *Olympus Heights* was out in October from Lily Poetry Review. He is co-editor of *Molecule: a tiny lit mag.* kevincareywriter.com

Jennifer Martelli (she, her, hers) is the author of *The Queen of Queens* (forthcoming, Bordighera Press) and *My Tarantella* (Bordighera Press), selected as a 2019 "Must Read" by the Massachusetts Center for the Book, chosen as a finalist for the Housatonic Book Award, and given an honorable mention from the Italian American Studies Association. She is also the author of the chapbooks *In the Year of Ferraro* from Nixes Mate Press and *After Bird*, winner of the Grey Book Press open reading. Her work has appeared in *The Tahoma Literary Review, The Sycamore Review, Thrush, Cream City Review, Verse Daily,*

Iron Horse Review (winner of the Photo Finish contest), *Poetry,* and elsewhere. Jennifer Martelli has twice received grants from the Massachusetts Cultural Council for her poetry. She is co-poetry editor for *Mom Egg Review* and co-curates the Italian American Writers Association Reading Series.

Stephenie Young is a photographer, writer and professor of comparative literature at Salem State University who is originally from Southern California. She has widely published her writing about trauma, war and social oppression, including a recent essay about the meme and fake news during Covid with Serbian visual artist Vladimir Miladinović, "The Reluctant Screen Shot Collector," for the *Journal of Visual Culture* and Harun Farocki Institute in London. Her current project is a multi-year photographic study of the disappearing world of Kurdistan. She has lived in Somerville, Massachusetts since 2008.

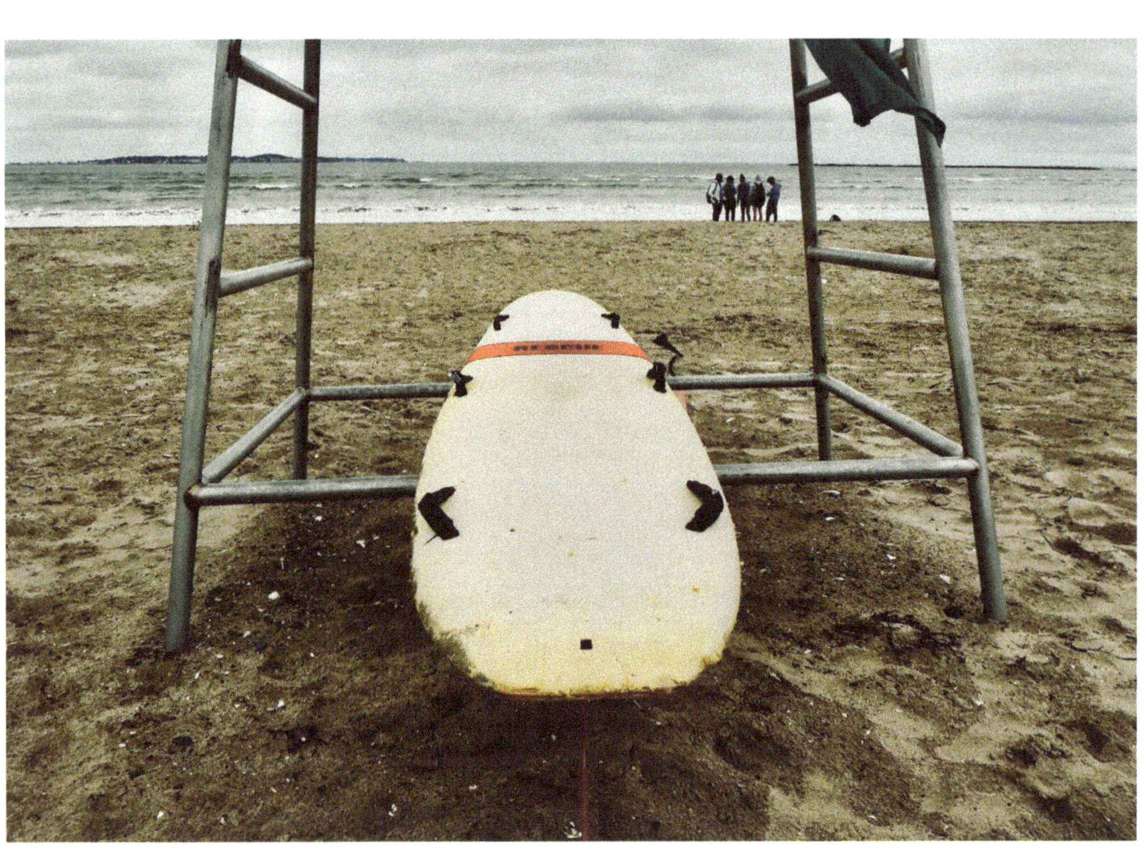

ACKNOWLEDGMENTS

1. "The Recipe," (in part) *The Beach People* / Red Bird Chapbooks
2. "The Devil Tides," *Lindenwood Review* (winner, prose poetry contest)
3. "the beach people doing beach things" (in part) *The Beach People* / Red Bird Chapbooks
4. "Always." *Jesus was a Homeboy* / Cavan Kerry Press
5. "Diving Horses" (in part) originally as "Revere Beach" *The Paterson Literary Review* and *The One Fifteen to Penn Station* / CavanKerry Press
6. "Tongue Root." *Luna Luna Magazine*
7. "Low-/Tide Heart of Mine." *r.kv.ry*
8. "As a Crow Flies." *Slippery Elm*
9. "I Sleep in the Daytime." *Muddy River Poetry Review*
10. "Strangers" (in part) originally as "Man on the Beach" *The One Fifteen to Penn Station* /CavanKerry Press
11. "The Veiled Women." *Poemeleon*
12 "A Long Line." *Set in Stone* / CavanKerry Press
13. "Metamorphosis." *Milk Cake Press*

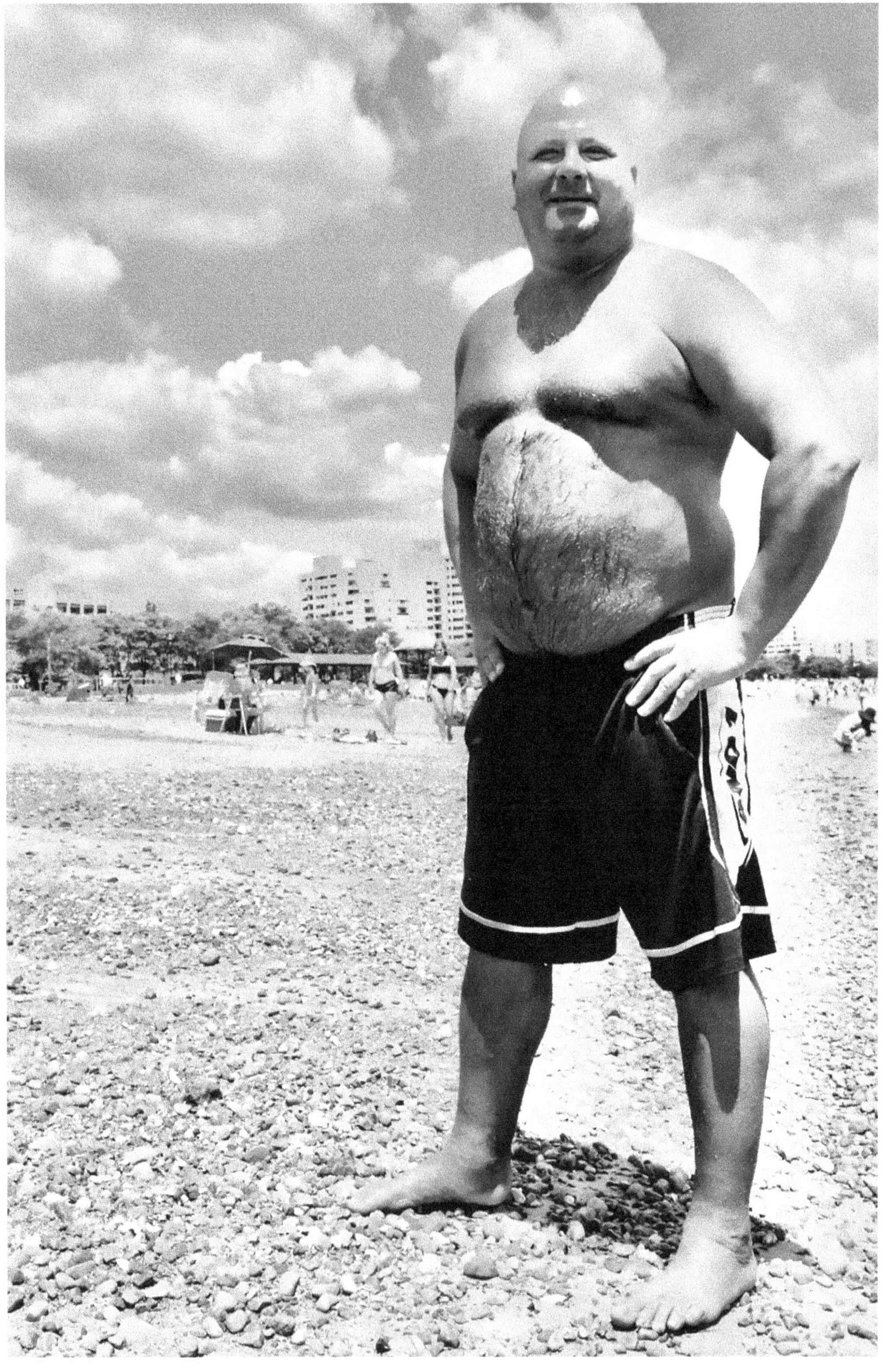

Red Nuns are navigational aids. Red. Right. Returning.

Nixes Mate is a navigational hazard in Boston Harbor.